EDGE
BOOKS™

MANX
Cats

by Joanne Mattern

CAPSTONE PRESS
a capstone imprint

Edge Books are published by Capstone Press,
151 Good Counsel Drive, P.O. Box 669, Mankato, Minnesota 56002.
www.capstonepub.com

Books published by Capstone Press are manufactured with paper
containing at least 10 percent post-consumer waste.

Library of Congress Cataloging-in-Publication Data
Mattern, Joanne, 1963–
  Manx cats / by Joanne Mattern.
    p. cm.—(Edge Books. All about cats)
  Includes bibliographical references and index.
  Summary: "Describes the history, physical features, temperament,
    and care of the Manx cat breed"—Provided by publisher.
  ISBN 978-1-4296-6632-9 (library binding)
  1. Manx cat—Juvenile literature. I. Title. II. Series.
  SF449.M36M383 2011
  636.8'22—dc22   2010042247

Editorial Credits
Connie R. Colwell and Anthony Wacholtz, editors; Heidi Thompson, designer;
    Wanda Winch, media researcher; Eric Manske, production specialist

Photo Credits
Corbis: Reuters/Eric Thayer, 12; Fox Hill Farm/Paulette Johnson, 9, 17, 23,
24, 25, 27, 28; iStockphoto: Cynthia Baldauf, 15, David Gilder, 11; Photo by
Fiona Green, 5, 6, 19, 21, 22; photolibrary/Peter Arnold: J-L. Klein & M-L.
Hubert, 18; Ron Kimball Stock: Klein-Hubert, 16, Ron Kimball, cover

Printed in the United States of America in Stevens Point, Wisconsin.
092010   005934WZS11

TABLE OF CONTENTS

Chapter 1

THE ROUND FELINE

No tail? No problem! The Manx is well known for being a tailless **breed**. In reality, the tails of Manx can be one of several types, from a full-grown tail to no tail at all. Manx with tails are sometimes mistaken as cats from another breed, but people can easily identify a tailless Manx.

The Manx is a medium-sized breed that can be longhaired or shorthaired. Its double coat makes it look bigger than it actually is. The Manx's back legs are longer than its front legs. The longer back legs make the back end stick up higher than the head. If the Manx doesn't have a tail, the back end has an oval shape. Add in circular cheeks and a broad head, and it's easy to see why the Manx is called the "rounded" cat.

breed—a certain kind of animal within an animal group; breed also means to mate and raise a certain kind of animal

Manx are well known for having round bodies and no tails.

The Manx is a popular breed in the Cat Fanciers' Association (CFA). The CFA is the world's largest cat **registry**. The CFA considers shorthaired and longhaired Manx as the same breed. But other cat registries consider longhaired Manx a separate breed called the Cymric.

The longhaired Manx has patches of longer hair on its neck and abdomen.

registry—an organization that keeps track of the ancestry for cats of a certain breed

IS A MANX RIGHT FOR YOU?

If you're looking for a quiet but playful pet, a Manx could be right for you. The cat's powerful back legs make it a natural jumper and a fast runner. Manx love to leap for toys or chase them around the room. The Manx is also known to have doglike habits, such as fetching an item for its owner or burying its toys. These cats also have the loyalty of a dog and become closely attached to their owners.

If you are interested in making a Manx your pet, you have several options. If you want a purebred Manx, you should visit a breeder. Most breeders register their cats and kittens. Registered cats have papers that list the names of the breeder, the cat's parents, and sometimes the cat's other relatives. A breeder can often show potential owners the parents of a kitten. The buyer can get an idea of how the kitten will look and behave when it becomes an adult.

You can also contact an animal shelter or rescue organization to adopt a Manx. Animal shelters can be inexpensive places to buy a cat. Shelters care for animals while trying to find homes for them. Rescue organizations also try to find homes for animals. Rescue organizations are similar to animal shelters, but they usually specialize in certain pet breeds. Pets from rescue organizations are usually less expensive than pets from breeders.

Chapter 2

MANX HISTORY

The Manx developed on the Isle of Man, an island between Great Britain and Ireland. It is the only cat bred specifically to have no tail. There are several **legends** that have tried to explain the origin of tailless cats.

WHERE DID THE TAIL GO?

One Manx legend involves the story of Noah's ark from the Bible. Noah was saving two of every animal from a great flood. The Manx was late getting onto the ark, and Noah was in a hurry to sail away. As the Manx came through the door, Noah accidentally slammed the ark's door on the cat's tail, cutting it off. All Manx from then on had no tails.

Another legend describes Viking warriors who invaded the Isle of Man in the 800s. These warriors decorated their helmets with animal tails. To keep their kittens safe, female Manx bit off their kittens' tails so the Vikings wouldn't kill them.

legend—a story handed down from earlier times

The Manx is one of the oldest cat breeds in Europe.

Yet another legend goes back to 1588, when ships from Spain attacked England. Some people think that tailless cats swam to the Isle of Man from one of the Spanish ships. However, there are no records of tailless cats in Spain.

HEREDITY AND GENETICS

Although Manx legends are entertaining, they are not true. The real story most likely involves **genes**. Most people think that a genetic **mutation** caused Manx to be born without tails. A genetic mutation causes part of an animal's body to develop in a different way than normal. The mutation can be passed down to the animal's offspring.

Animals that lived on the Isle of Man had little contact with animals from other parts of the world. Therefore the tailless mutation was able to spread throughout the entire cat population. More and more cats inherited the mutation and were born without tails.

gene—the part of a cell that carries information about how a living thing will look and behave

mutation—a change in an animal's genes that results in a new characteristic or trait

Manx kittens inherit the tailless gene from their parents.

A shorthair Manx named Cali won an award at a 2006 cat show at Madison Square Garden in New York.

GAINING POPULARITY

Records of Manx on the Isle of Man begin about 300 years ago. In 1810 British painter Joseph Turner wrote that he had seven Manx that came from the Isle of Man.

People first displayed Manx in European cat shows in the 1870s. Many of the show cats had an uneven, hopping walk because their back legs were longer than their front legs. Today breeders try to breed cats that walk normally.

A shorthaired Manx first competed at a U.S. cat show in 1899. In 1958 a Manx named Mrs. Kelly of An-Si became the first Manx to win a CFA Grand Champion title. In 1989 longhaired Manx were allowed to participate in cat shows. Today both longhaired and shorthaired Manx are popular show cats.

FACT: The CFA officially recognized the Manx breed around 1920.

Chapter 3

THE MANY LOOKS OF A MANX

Today's Manx look very much like the Manx of 300 years ago. These round, powerful cats often live long, healthy lives. Manx can live 15 years or more with proper care.

Although the Manx looks big, it is a medium-sized cat. Most males weigh between 10 and 13 pounds (4.5 and 5.9 kilograms). Females are a little smaller, weighing between 7 and 11 pounds (3.2 and 5 kg).

Manx have round heads and puffy cheeks. The breed can have either a long or short coat, but all Manx have a double coat of fur. The undercoat is dense and soft, while the outer coat is glossy and smooth.

The back legs of a Manx are longer than its front legs. The cat's back curves up toward its muscular hind legs. Manx have an incredible jumping ability because of their powerful back legs. These cats are also fast runners and can quickly change directions.

 **FACT:** Manx have been called "race car cats" because of their speed and ability to make sharp turns.

Cat trees are perfect for Manx. The cats can jump to one of the platforms and perch high off the ground.

TAIL TYPES

A Manx is often described by its tail type. A Manx can have a long tail, a stumpy tail, a riser tail, or no tail. The cats are nicknamed by the type of tail they have. Manx with full tails are called longies, while cats with short, stumpy tails are called stumpies. Manx with no tails are called rumpies.

Rumpies have a small indent at the end of their spine where a tail would be.

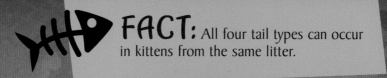

Manx with a bump at the end of their spine are also called rumpy-risers.

The last type of Manx are known as risers. These cats have a small bump of **cartilage** where the tail normally starts. Rumpies and risers are the only types of Manx that can compete at cat shows.

cartilage—a strong, rubbery tissue that connects bones in most animals

COLORS

The fur of a Manx comes in almost every color and pattern. Common colors are white, black, cream, silver, blue, and red. Tabby, calico, and tortoiseshell coats also are common. Calico cats are white with black and red patches. The coats of tortoiseshell cats may have a few white markings but are mostly black and red.

tabby—a striped coat

The coats of calico cats have a mixture of black, red, and white.

PERSONALITY

Manx are known as a playful breed. They seem to prefer toys that allow them to be active. On top of being athletic, Manx are also smart. Some Manx can learn commands and how to open doors.

Manx are social cats. They get along well with children and enjoy being around other cats and dogs. These cats are loyal and often seek attention. Many Manx become very close to their owners.

Chapter 4

CARING FOR A MANX

Manx are considered to be a healthy breed. Like other cats, Manx should be kept indoors. Outdoor cats have a greater chance of getting a disease than cats that are kept indoors. Cats that roam around outside are also in danger of being hit by cars or attacked by other animals.

FEEDING

Manx need well-balanced diets to stay healthy and strong. Supermarkets and pet stores sell high-quality cat food that provides a healthy diet.

When it comes to feeding your Manx, you can choose dry or moist food. Dry food is usually less expensive than moist food. It does not spoil if it is left out for long periods of time. The rough texture of dry food helps clean cats' teeth. Moist food should not be left out for more than one hour because it can spoil easily. If you are unsure which type of food to give your cat, you should ask a veterinarian for advice.

Putting out a specific amount of food
will ensure that your cat won't overeat.

Manx should always have plenty of water available. You should routinely check to make sure their bowl is filled with fresh, clean water.

GROOMING

Shorthaired Manx need little grooming and only need to be brushed once a week. Longhaired Manx should be brushed daily. Use a soft bristle brush to remove any loose hair. After you finish brushing, use a comb to smooth out the cat's fur. Good grooming can help keep your Manx from developing **hairballs**.

Use long, slow strokes when you brush your Manx's coat.

LITTER BOXES

Every cat needs access to a **litter** box. Cats use litter boxes to get rid of bodily waste. Cats are clean animals and may refuse to use a dirty litter box. You should use a scoop to remove waste from the box each day. Replace the litter about every two weeks. You should change it more often if most of the litter is wet or lumpy.

hairball—a ball of fur that lodges in a cat's stomach

litter—small bits of clay or other material used to absorb the waste of cats and other animals

23

DENTAL CARE

All cats need regular dental care to protect their teeth and gums from **plaque**. Cats should have their teeth brushed at least once each week. Use a toothbrush and toothpaste made for cats. You can also use a soft cloth that is gentle on cats' gums. Never use a toothpaste that is made for people. It can make your cat sick.

You may need to use your other hand to keep your cat's head still while you brush its teeth.

plaque—a coating of germs and saliva on teeth that can cause tooth decay

24

NAIL CARE

A Manx should have its nails trimmed every few weeks. Cats with trimmed nails are less likely to damage carpet or furniture. They are also less likely to develop an infection from an ingrown nail.

The easiest way to get your cat used to having its nails cut is to start when it is a kitten. The cat will get used to having its nails trimmed by the time it is an adult.

Some people go to the veterinarian to get their cats declawed. However, these surgeries are permanent and leave cats defenseless if they end up outdoors. The CFA and other cat organizations recommend that people avoid declawing their cats.

You can reduce the chance of hurting your Manx when trimming its nails by using nail clippers made for cats.

FACT: When cats sharpen their claws on scratching posts, the old part of the nail falls off.

SCRATCHING POSTS

Like other cats, Manx like to scratch for a variety of reasons. Cats mark their territories by leaving their scent on objects they scratch. They also scratch to release tension and keep their claws sharp. You should provide your Manx with a scratching post so that it won't scratch the carpet, furniture, or curtains. You can buy a scratching post at a pet store. You can also ask an adult to help you make one from wood and carpet.

HEALTH CARE

Manx should be checked yearly by a veterinarian. The vet will check the cat's heart, lungs, eyes, ears, and mouth. Depending on the cat's medical history, it may need **vaccinations**. Kittens often have their first vaccinations when they are about 10 weeks old. Vaccinations help prevent diseases such as rabies and feline leukemia.

vaccination—a shot of medicine that protects animals from a disease

Scratching posts allow kittens to sharpen their claws without damaging furniture.

To take a cat's temperature, vets can use a special thermometer that goes in the cat's ear.

Rabies is a deadly disease that is spread by animal bites. Many states have laws that require owners to vaccinate their cats against rabies. Feline leukemia attacks a cat's immune system. The cat is unable to fight off infections and other illnesses. Cats should receive some vaccinations each year, while other vaccinations are given less often.

Vets also can spay and neuter cats. These surgeries make it impossible for cats to breed, which helps control the pet population. The surgeries also help protect against certain diseases. Spayed and neutered cats usually have calmer personalities than cats that do not have the surgeries. You should have your Manx spayed or neutered if you don't plan to breed it.

With its playful and lively nature, a Manx makes a great family pet. The breed's sweet personality can brighten anyone's day. Tail or no tail, a Manx makes a lovable, loyal companion.

GLOSSARY

breed (BREED)—a certain kind of animal within an animal group; breed also means to mate and raise a certain kind of animal

cartilage (KAHR-tuh-lij)—a strong, rubbery tissue that connects bones in most animals

gene (JEEN)—the part of a cell that carries information about how a living thing will look and behave

hairball (HAIR-bawl)—a ball of fur that lodges in a cat's stomach

legend (LEJ-uhnd)—a story handed down over time

litter (LIT-ur)—small bits of clay or other material used to absorb the waste of cats and other animals

mutation (myoo-TAY-shun)—a change in an animal's genes that results in a new characteristic or trait

plaque (PLAK)—the coating of food, saliva, and bacteria that forms on teeth and can cause tooth decay

registry (REH-juh-stree)—an organization that keeps track of the ancestry for cats of a certain breed

tabby (TAB-ee)—a striped coat

vaccination (vak-suh-NAY-shun)—a shot of medicine that protects animals from a disease

READ MORE

Britton, Tamara L. *Manx Cats*. Cats. Edina, Minn.: ABDO Publishing Company, 2011.

Jenkins, Steve. *Dogs and Cats*. Boston: Houghton Mifflin Company, 2007.

Rau, Dana Meachen. *Top 10 Cats for Kids.* Top Pets for Kids With American Humane. Berkeley Heights, N.J.: Enslow Elementary, 2009.

INTERNET SITES

FactHound offers a safe, fun way to find Internet sites related to this book. All of the sites on FactHound have been researched by our staff.

Here's all you do:

Visit *www.facthound.com*

Type in this code: 9781429666329

Check out projects, games and lots more at
www.capstonekids.com

INDEX